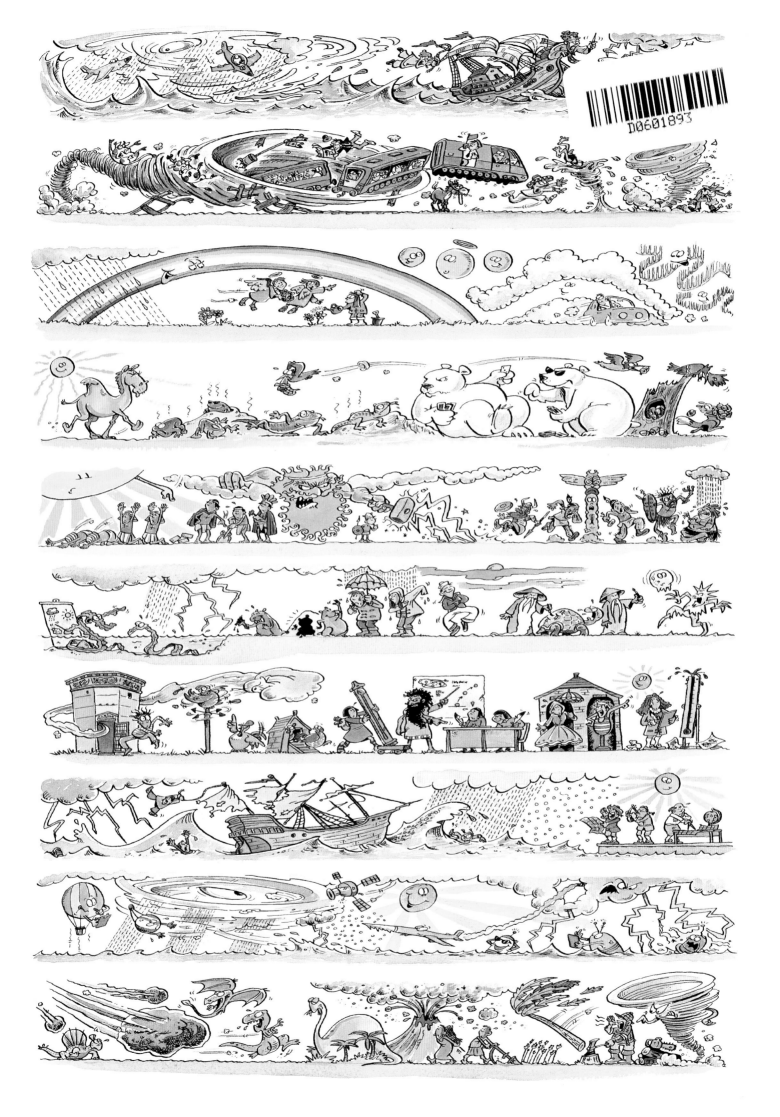

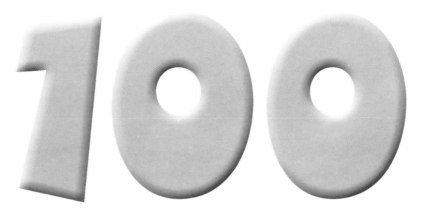

things you should know about

WEATHER

100

things you should know about

WEATHER

Clare Oliver

Consultant: Clive Carpenter

BARNES
&NOBLE
BOOKS
NEW YORK

First published in 2001 by Miles Kelly Publishing Ltd,
Bardfield Centre, Great Bardfield, Essex, CM7 4SL, U.K.

Copyright © Miles Kelly Publishing 2003

This edition published by Barnes & Noble, Inc.

2 4 6 8 10 9 7 5 3 1

Editorial Director: Anne Marshall
Editors: Amanda Learmonth, Jenni Rainford
Design: John Christopher
Indexing, Proof Reading: Jane Parker, Lynn Bresler
Americanization: Sean Connolly

Library of Congress Cataloging-in-Publication Data on file
at the Library of Congress

2004 Barnes & Noble Books

ISBN 0-7607-5393-8

Printed and bound in China

ACKNOWLEDGMENTS
The publishers would like to thank the following artists who have
contributed to this book:

Mark Bergin
Kuo Kang Chen
Steve Caldwell
Nicholas Forder
Chris Forsey
Terry Gabbey
Shammi Ghale
Alan Hancocks
Alan Harris
Kevin Maddison

Janos Marffy
Rachel Phillips
Martin Sanders
Peter Sarson
Sarah Smith
Rudi Vizi
Steve Weston
Tony Wilkins

Cartoons by Mark Davis at Mackerel

Contents

What is weather? 6

The four seasons 8

Fewer seasons 10

What a scorcher! 12

Our atmosphere 14

Clouds and rain 16

Not just fluffy 18

Flood warning 20

Deep freeze 22

When the wind blows 24

Thunderbolts and lightning 26

Eye of the hurricane 28

Wild whirling winds 30

Pretty lights 32

Made for weather 34

Weather myths 36

Rain or shine? 38

Instruments and inventors 40

World of weather 42

Weather watch 44

Changing climate 46

Index 48

What is weather?

1 **Rain, sunshine, snow, and storms are all types of weather.** These help us decide what clothes we wear, what food we eat, and what kind of life we lead. Weather also affects how animals and plants survive. Different types of weather are caused by what is happening in the atmosphere, the air above our heads. In some parts of the world, the weather changes every day; in others, it is nearly always the same.

Equator

2 **Tropical, temperate, and polar are all types of climate.** Climate is the name we give to patterns of weather over a period of time. Near the Equator, the weather is mostly hot and steamy. We call this a tropical climate. Near the North and South Poles, ice lies on the ground year-round and there are biting-cold blizzards. This is a polar climate. Most of the world has a temperate climate, with a mix of cold and warm seasons.

Mountainous

Desert

North Pole

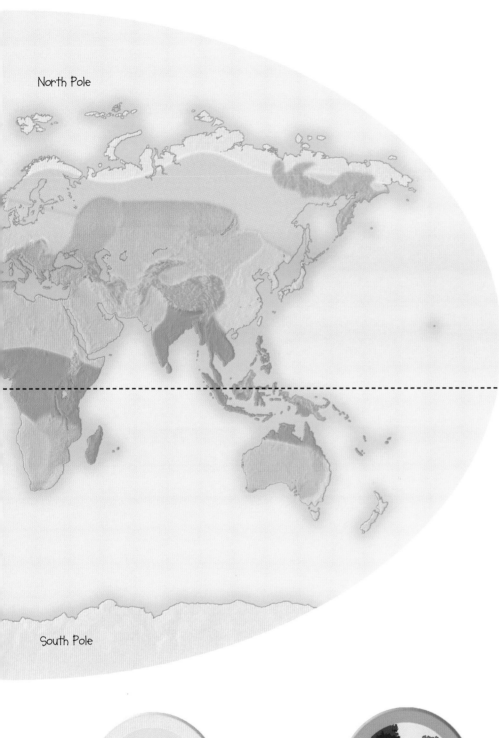

South Pole

Cold temperate

Wet temperate

Dry temperate

Polar

Tropical

▲ Look at the colored rings to match the different climate scenes to the main map. In general, the warmest climates are found close to the Equator, an imaginary line around the middle of the world. The closer to the Poles, the cooler the climate.

The four seasons

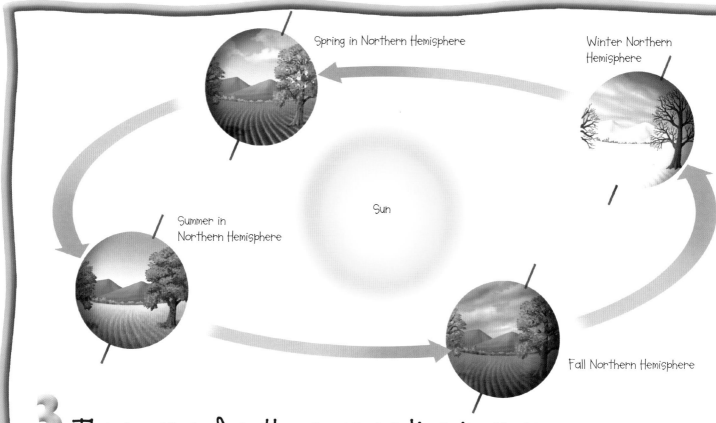

Spring in Northern Hemisphere

Winter Northern Hemisphere

Summer in Northern Hemisphere

Sun

Fall Northern Hemisphere

3 **The reason for the seasons lies in space.**
Our planet Earth plots a path through space that takes it around the Sun. This path, or orbit, takes one year. The Earth is tilted, so over the year first one and then the other Pole leans toward the Sun, giving us seasons. In June, for example, the North Pole leans toward the Sun. The Sun heats the northern half of Earth and there is summer.

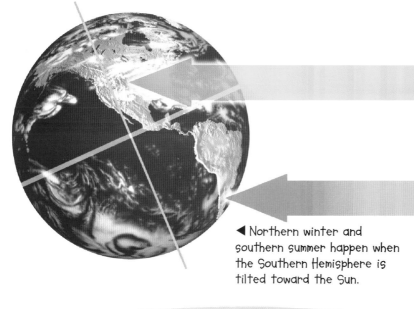

◄ Northern winter and southern summer happen when the Southern Hemisphere is tilted toward the Sun.

4 **When it is summer in Argentina, it is winter in Canada.** In December, the South Pole leans toward the Sun. Places in the southern half of the world, such as Argentina, have summer. At the same time, places in the northern half, such as Canada, have winter.

5 A day can last 21 hours!

Night and day happen because Earth is spinning as it circles the Sun. At the height of summer, places near the North Pole are so tilted toward the Sun that it is light almost all day long. In Stockholm, Sweden, Midsummer's Eve lasts 21 hours because the Sun disappears below the horizon for only three hours.

▲ At the North Pole, the Sun never disappears below the horizon at Midsummer's Day.

▼ Deciduous trees like these lose their leaves in the fall, but evergreens keep their leaves all year round.

I DON'T BELIEVE IT!

When the Sun shines all day in the far north, there is 24-hour night in the far south.

6 Forests change color in the fall.

Fall comes between summer and winter. Trees prepare for the cold winter months ahead by losing their leaves. First, though, they suck back the precious green chlorophyll, or dye, in their leaves, making them turn glorious shades of red, orange, and brown.

Fewer seasons

7 **Monsoons are winds that carry heavy rains.** The rains fall in the tropics in summer during the hot, rainy season. The Sun warms up the sea, which causes huge banks of cloud to form. Monsoons then blow these clouds toward land. Once the rains hit the continent, they can pour for weeks.

▶ When the rains are especially heavy, they cause chaos. Streets turn to rivers and sometimes people's homes are even washed away.

I DON'T BELIEVE IT !

In parts of monsoon India, more than 1,000in (2,500cm) of rain have fallen in a single year!

8 **Monsoons happen mainly in Asia.** However, there are some parts of the Americas that are close to the Equator that also have a season that is very rainy. Winds can carry such heavy rain clouds that there are flash floods in the deserts of the southwestern United States. The floods happen because the land has been baked hard during the dry season.

9 **Many parts of the tropics have two seasons, not four.** They are the parts of the world closest to the Equator, an imaginary line around the middle of the Earth. Here it is always hot, as these places are constantly facing the Sun. However, the movement of the Earth affects the position of a great band of cloud. In June, the tropical areas north of the Equator have the strongest heat and the heaviest rainstorms. In December, it is the turn of the areas south of the Equator.

Tropic of Cancer

Equator

Tropic of Capricorn

▲ The tropics lie either side of the Equator, between lines of latitude called the Tropic of Cancer and the Tropic of Capricorn.

10 **In a tropical rain forest, you need your umbrella every day!** Rain forests have rainy weather all year round—but there is still a wet and a dry season. It is just that the wet season is even wetter!

▼ Daily rainfall feeds the lush rain forest vegetation.

What a scorcher!

11 **All our heat comes from the Sun.** The Sun is a star, a super-hot ball of burning gases. It gives off heat rays that travel 93 million mi (150 million km) through space to our planet. Over the journey, the rays cool down, but they can still scorch the Earth.

QUIZ

1. How many seasons are there in the tropics?
2. On which continent do most monsoons occur?
3. Where is the hottest recorded place in the world?
4. Is El Niño a wind or a current?

1.Two 2.Asia 3.Al Aziziyah in Libya 4.A current

12 **The Sahara is the sunniest place.** This North African desert once had 4,300 hours of sunshine in a year! People who live there, such as the Tuareg Arabs, cover their skin to avoid being sunburned.

13 **The hottest place on Earth is Al Aziziyah in Libya.** It is 136°F (58°C) in the shade —hot enough to fry an egg!

▶ Desert peoples wear headdresses to protect their skin and eyes from the sun and sand.

▼ A mirage is just a trick of the light. It can make us see something that is not really there.

14 The Sun can trick your eyes.

Sometimes, as sunlight passes through our atmosphere, it hits layers of air at different temperatures. When this happens, the air bends the light and can trick our eyes into seeing something that is not there. This is a mirage. For example, what looks like a pool of water might really be part of the sky reflected on to the land.

15 Too much sun brings drought.

Clear skies and sunshine are not always good news. Without rain crops wither, and people and their animals go hungry.

16 One terrible drought made a "Dust Bowl."

Settlers in the midwest were ruined by a long drought during the 1930s. As crops died, there were no roots to hold the soil together. The dry earth turned to dust and some farms simply blew away!

▶ The "Dust Bowl" was caused by strong winds and dust storms. These destroyed huge areas of land.

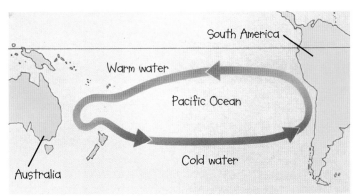

17 A sea current can set forests alight.

All sorts of things affect our weather and climate. The movements of a sea current called El Niño have been blamed for causing terrible droughts—which led to unstoppable forest fires.

◀ El Niño has been known to cause violent weather conditions. It returns on average every four years.

Our atmosphere

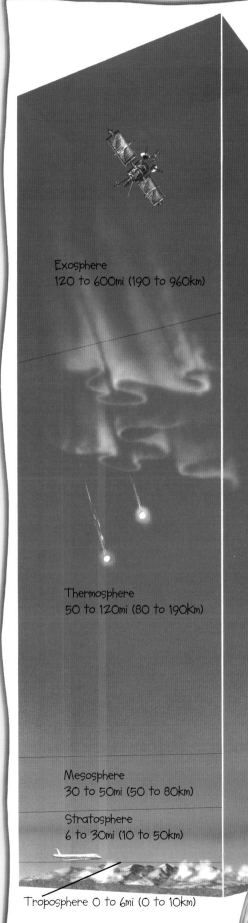

Exosphere
120 to 600mi (190 to 960km)

Thermosphere
50 to 120mi (80 to 190km)

Mesosphere
30 to 50mi (50 to 80km)

Stratosphere
6 to 30mi (10 to 50km)

Troposphere 0 to 6mi (0 to 10km)

18 **Our planet is wrapped in a blanket of air.** We call this blanket the atmosphere. It stretches hundreds of miles above our heads. The blanket keeps in heat, especially at night when part of the planet faces away from the Sun. During the day, the blanket becomes a sunscreen instead. Without an atmosphere, there would be no weather.

19 **Most weather happens in the troposphere.** This is the layer of atmosphere that stretches from the ground to around 6mi (10km) above your head. The higher in the troposphere you go, the cooler the air. Because of this, clouds are most likely to form here. Clouds with flattened tops show just where the troposphere meets the next layer, the stratosphere.

◄ The atmosphere stretches right into space. Scientists have split it into five layers, or spheres, such as the troposphere.

▼ The Earth is surrounded by the atmosphere. It acts as a blanket, protecting us from the Sun's fierce rays.

20 Air just cannot keep still. Tiny particles in air, called molecules, are always bumping into each other! The more they smash into each other, the greater the air pressure. Generally, there are more smashes lower in the troposphere, because the pull of gravity makes the molecules fall toward the Earth's surface. The higher you go, the lower the air pressure, and the less oxygen there is in the air.

▶ At high altitudes there is less oxygen. That is why mountaineers often wear breathing equipment.

High pressure

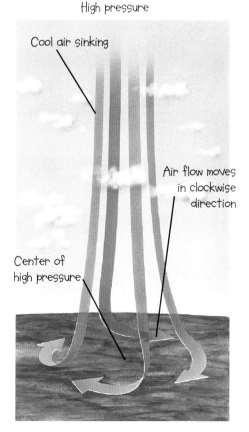

Cool air sinking

Air flow moves in clockwise direction

Center of high pressure

Low pressure

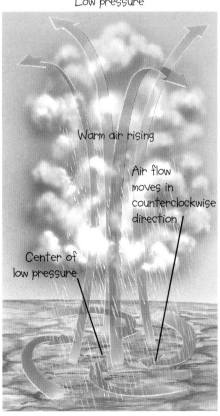

Warm air rising

Air flow moves in counterclockwise direction

Center of low pressure

21 Warmth makes air move. When heat from the Sun warms the molecules in air, they move faster and spread out more. This makes the air lighter, so it rises in the sky, creating low pressure. As it gets higher, the air cools. The molecules slow down and become heavier again, so they start to sink back to Earth.

◀ A high pressure weather system gives us warmer weather, while low pressure gives us cooler more unsettled weather.

Clouds and rain

22 **Rain comes from the sea.** As the Sun heats the surface of the ocean, some seawater turns into water vapor and rises into the air. As it rises, it cools and turns back into water droplets. Lots of water droplets make clouds. The droplets join together to make bigger and bigger drops that eventually fall as rain. Some rain is soaked up by the land, but a lot finds its way back to the sea. This is called the water cycle.

▶ The water cycle involves all the water on Earth. Water vapor rises from lakes, rivers, and the sea to form clouds in the atmosphere.

RAIN GAUGE
You will need:
glass jar waterproof marker pen
ruler notebook   pen
Put the jar outside. At the same time each day, mark the rainwater level on the jar with your pen. At the end of a week, empty the jar. Measure and record how much rain fell each day and over the whole week.

23 Some mountains are so tall that their summits (peaks) are hidden by cloud. Really huge mountains even affect the weather. When moving air hits a mountain slope it is forced upward. As it travels up, the temperature drops, and clouds form.

◀ Warm, rising air may be forced up the side of a mountain. At a certain level, lower temperatures make the water form clouds.

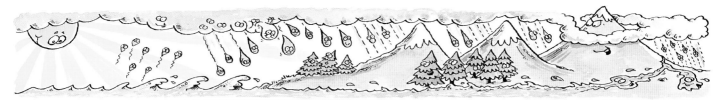

Rain falls, filling rivers

Water is given off by forests

Clouds form

The rivers run back to the sea, and the cycle starts again

Water evaporates from the sea

▼ Virga happens when rain reaches a layer of dry air. The rain droplets turn back into water vapor in midair, and seem to disappear.

24
Some rain never reaches the ground. The raindrops turn back into water vapor because they hit a layer of super-dry air. You can actually see the drops falling like a curtain from the cloud, but the curtain stops in midair. This type of weather is called virga.

25
Clouds gobble up heat and keep the Earth's temperature regular. From each 6 ft sq (2 m sq) patch of land, clouds can remove the equivalent energy created by a 60-Watt lightbulb.

Not just fluffy

26 **Clouds come in all shapes and sizes.**
To help recognize them, scientists split them into ten basic types. The type depends on what the cloud looks like and where it forms in the sky. Cirrus clouds look like wisps of smoke. They form high in the troposphere and rarely mean rain. Stratus clouds form in flat layers and may produce drizzle or a sprinkling of snow. All types of cumulus clouds bring rain. Some are huge cauliflower shapes. They look soft and fluffy—but would feel soggy to touch.

Cumulonimbus clouds give heavy rain showers

▶ The main classes of cloud—cirrus, cumulus, and stratus—were named in the 1800s. An amateur British weather scientist named Luke Howard identified the different types.

27 **Not all clouds produce rain.** Cumulus humilis clouds are the smallest heap-shaped clouds. In the sky, they look like lumpy, cotton wool sausages! They are too small to produce rain but they can grow into much bigger, rain-carrying cumulus clouds. The biggest cumulus clouds, cumulus congestus, bring heavy showers.

Cumulus clouds bring rain

Cirrus clouds occur at great heights from the ground

Cirrostratus

Contrails are the white streaks created by planes

28

Sometimes the sky is filled with white patches of cloud that look like shimmering fish scales. These are called mackerel skies. It takes lots of gusty wind to break the cloud into these little patches, and so mackerel skies are usually a sign of changeable weather.

29

Not all clouds are made by nature. Contrails are streaky clouds that a plane leaves behind it as it flies. They are made of water vapor that comes from the plane's engines. The second it hits the cold air, the vapor turns into ice crystals, leaving a trail of white snow cloud.

Stratus clouds can bring drizzle or appear as fog

MIX AND MATCH

Can you match the names of these five types of clouds to their meanings?

1. Altostratus   a. heap
2. Cirrus   b. layer
3. Cumulonimbus   c. high + layer
4. Cumulus   d. wisp
5. Stratus   e. heap + rain

1c 2d 3e 4a 5b

Flood warning

▲ Flooding can cause great damage to buildings and the countryside.

30 **Too much rain brings floods.** There are two different types of floods. Flash floods happen after a short burst of heavy rainfall, usually caused by thunderstorms. Broadscale flooding happens when rain falls steadily over a wide area—for weeks or months—without stopping. When this happens, rivers slowly fill and eventually burst their banks. Tropical storms, such as hurricanes, can also lead to broadscale flooding.

31 **There can be floods in the desert.** When a lot of rain falls very quickly on to land that has been baked dry, it cannot soak in. Instead, it sits on the surface, causing flash floods.

◀ A desert flash flood can create streams of muddy brown water. After the water level falls, vegetation bursts into life.

32 **There really was a Great Flood.** The Bible tells of a terrible flood, and how a man called Noah was saved. Recently, explorers found the first real evidence of the Flood—a sunken beach 460ft (140m) below the surface of the Black Sea. There are ruins of houses, dating back to 5600BC. Stories of a huge flood in ancient times do not appear only in the Bible—the Babylonians and Greeks told of one, too.

▲ In the Bible story, Noah survived the Great Flood by building a huge wooden boat called an ark.

33 **Mud can flood.** When rain mixes with earth it makes mud. On bare mountainsides, there are no tree roots to hold the soil together. An avalanche of mud can slide off the mountain. The worst-ever mudslide happened after flooding in Colombia, South America, in 1985. It buried 23,000 people from the town of Armero.

▼ Mudslides can devastate whole towns and villages, as the flow of mud covers everything it meets.

I DON'T BELIEVE IT!

The ancient Egyptians had a story to explain the yearly flooding of the Nile. They said the goddess Isis filled the river with tears, as she cried for her lost husband.

Deep freeze

34 Snow is made of tiny ice crystals. When air temperatures are very cold—around 32°F (0°C)—the water droplets in the clouds freeze to make tiny ice crystals. Sometimes, individual crystals fall, but usually they clump together into snowflakes.

I DON'T BELIEVE IT!

Antarctica is the coldest place on Earth. Temperatures of –128.6°F (–89.2°C) have been recorded there.

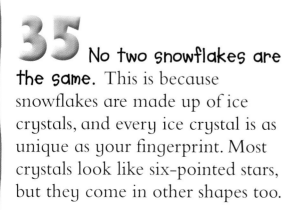

35 No two snowflakes are the same. This is because snowflakes are made up of ice crystals, and every ice crystal is as unique as your fingerprint. Most crystals look like six-pointed stars, but they come in other shapes too.

▲ Falling snow is made worse by strong winds, which can form deep drifts.

▶ Ice crystals seen under a microscope. A snowflake that is an inch or so across will be made up of lots of crystals like these.

▶ An avalanche gathers speed as it thunders down the mountainside.

38 **Avalanches are like giant snowballs.** They happen after lots of snow falls on a mountain. The slightest movement or sudden noise can jolt the pile of snow and start it moving down the slope. As it crashes down, the avalanche picks up extra snow and can end up large enough to bury whole towns.

39 **Marksmen shoot at snowy mountains.** One way to prevent deadly avalanches is to stop too much snow from building up. In mountain areas, marksmen set off mini avalanches on purpose. They make sure people are out of the danger zone, then fire guns to trigger a snowslide.

36 **Ice can stay frozen for millions of years.** At the North and South Poles, the weather never warms up enough for the ice to thaw. When fresh snow falls, it presses down on the snow already there, forming thick sheets. Some ice may not have melted for a million years or more.

37 **Black ice is not really black.** Drizzle or rain turns to ice when it touches freezing-cold ground. This "black" ice is see-through, and hard to spot against a road's dark asphalt. It is also terribly slippery—like a deadly ice rink.

▲ Antarctica is a frozen wilderness. The ice piles up to form amazing shapes, like this arch.

When the wind blows

40 **Wind is moving air.** Winds blow because air is constantly moving from areas of high pressure to areas of low pressure. The bigger the difference in temperature between the two areas, the faster the wind blows.

▶ These trees have been forced into strange shapes by the wind.

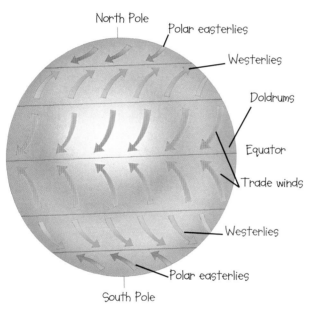

North Pole
Polar easterlies
Westerlies
Doldrums
Equator
Trade winds
Westerlies
Polar easterlies
South Pole

▲ This map shows the pattern of the world's main winds.

41 **Trade winds blow one way north of the Equator, and another way in the south.** Trade winds blow in the tropics, where air is moving to an area of low pressure at the Equator. Their name comes from their importance to traders, when goods traveled by sailing ship.

42 **Winds have names.** World wind patterns are called global winds. The most famous are the trade winds that blow toward the Equator. There are also well-known local winds, such as the cold, dry mistral that blows down to southern France, or the hot, dry sirroco that blows north of the Sahara.

QUIZ
1. At what temperature does water freeze?
2. What does the Beaufort Scale measure?
3. What are the mistral and sirroco?
4. How many sides does an ice crystal usually have?

1. 32°F (0°C)
2. Wind strength
3. Local winds 4. Six

43

You can tell how windy it is by looking at the leaves on a tree. Wind ranges from light breezes to hurricanes. Its strength is measured on the Beaufort Scale, named after the Irish admiral who devised it. The scale ranges from Force 0, meaning total calm, to Force 12, which is a hurricane.

Force 0: Calm

Force 1: Light air

Force 2: Light breeze

Force 3: Gentle breeze

Force 4: Moderate breeze

▶ The Beaufort Scale.

Force 5: Fresh breeze

Force 6: Strong breeze

Force 7: Near gale

Force 8: Gale

Force 9: Strong gale

Force 10: Storm

Force 11: Violent storm

Force 12: Hurricane

44

Wind can turn on your TV. People can harness the energy of the wind to make electricity for our homes. Tall turbines are positioned in windy spots. As the wind turns the turbine, the movement powers a generator and produces electrical energy.

45

Wind can make you mad! The Föhn wind, which blows across Switzerland, Austria, and Bavaria in southern Germany, brings with it changeable weather. This has been blamed for road accidents and even bouts of madness!

Thunderbolts and lightning

46 **Thunderstorms are most likely in summer.** Hot weather creates warm, moist air that rises and forms towering cumulonimbus clouds. Inside each cloud, water droplets and ice crystals bang about, building up positive and negative electrical charges. Electricity flows between the charges, creating a flash that heats the air around it. Lightning is so hot that it makes the air expand, making a loud noise or thunderclap. Cloud-to-cloud lightning is called sheet lightning, while lightning traveling from the cloud to the ground is called fork lightning.

47 **Lightning comes in different colors.** If there is rain in the thundercloud, the lightning looks red; if there's hail, it looks blue. Lightning can also be yellow or white.

▼ Lightning conductors absorb the shock and protect tall buildings.

▶ Dramatic lightning flashes light up the sky.

48 **Tall buildings are protected from lightning.** Church steeples and other tall structures are often struck by bolts of lightning. This could damage the building, or give electric shocks to people inside, so lightning conductors are placed on the roof. These channel the lightning safely away.

HOW CLOSE?

Lightning and thunder happen at the same time, but light travels faster than sound. Count the seconds between the flash and the clap and divide them by five (divide by three for kilometers). This is how many miles away the storm is.

49 **A person can survive a lightning strike.** Lightning is very dangerous and can give a big enough shock to kill you. However, an American park ranger named Roy Sullivan survived being struck seven times.

▼ A sudden hail storm can leave the ground littered with small chunks of ice.

50 **Hailstones can be as big as melons!** These chunks of ice can fall from thunderclouds. The biggest ever fell in Gopaljang, Bangladesh, in 1986 and weighed 2lb (1kg) each!

Eye of the hurricane

51 **Some winds travel at speeds of more than 70mph (120km/h).** Violent tropical storms happen when strong winds blow into an area of low pressure and start spinning very fast. They develop over warm seas and pick up speed until they reach land, where there is no more moist sea air to feed them. Such storms bring torrential rain.

52 **The center of a hurricane is calm and still.** This part is called the "eye." As the eye of the storm passes over, there is a pause in the terrifying rains and wind.

▼ This satellite photograph of a hurricane shows how the storm whirls around a central, still "eye."

▶ A Hurricane Hunter heads into the storm.

I DON'T BELIEVE IT !
Tropical storms are called different names. Hurricanes develop over the Atlantic, typhoons over the Pacific, and cyclones over the Indian Ocean.

53 **Hurricane Hunters fly close to the eye of a hurricane.** These are special weather planes that fly into the storm in order to take measurements. It is a dangerous job for the pilots, but the information they gather helps to predict the hurricane's path—and saves lives.

54 **Hurricanes have names.** One of the worst hurricanes was Hurricane Andrew, which battered the coast of Florida in 1992. Perhaps there is a hurricane named after you!

55 **Hurricanes whip up wild waves.** As the storm races over the ocean, the winds create giant waves. These hit the shore as a huge sea surge. In 1961, the sea surge following Hurricane Hattie washed away Belize City in Central America.

56 **Typhoons saved the Japanese from Genghis Khan.** The 13th-century Mongol leader made two attempts to invade Japan—and both times, a terrible typhoon battered his fleet and saved the Japanese!

▶ A typhoon prevented Genghis Khan's navy from invading Japan.

Wild whirling winds

57 **Tornadoes spin at speeds of 300mph (480km/h)!** These whirling columns of wind, also known as twisters, are some of the most destructive storms on Earth. They form in strong thunderstorms, when the back part of the thundercloud starts spinning. The spinning air forms a funnel that reaches down toward the Earth. When it touches the ground, it becomes a tornado.

58 **A tornado can be strong enough to lift a train!** The spinning tornado whizzes along the ground like an enormous, high-speed vacuum cleaner, sucking up everything in its path. It rips the roofs off houses, and even tosses buildings into the air. In the 1930s, a twister in Minnesota threw a train car full of people more than 25ft (7m) through the air!

▶ A tornado can cause great damage to anything in its path.

59 Tornado Alley is a twister hotspot in the American midwest. This is where hot air traveling north from the Gulf of Mexico meets cold polar winds traveling south, and creates huge thunderclouds. Of course, tornadoes can happen anywhere in the world when the conditions are right.

Minneapolis
Sioux Falls
Chicago
Denver
Kansas City
St. Louis
Wichita
U. S. A.
Amarillo
Oklahoma City
Dallas
New Orleans
Houston
MEXICO

▲ The shaded area shows Tornado Alley, where there are hundreds of tornadoes each year.

60 A pillar of whirling water can rise out of a lake or the sea. Waterspouts are spiraling columns of water that can be sucked up by a tornado as it forms over a lake or the sea. They tend to spin more slowly than tornadoes, because water is much heavier than air.

▲ Waterspouts can suck up fish living in a lake!

I DON'T BELIEVE IT!

Loch Ness in Scotland is famous for sightings of a monster nicknamed Nessie. Perhaps people who have seen Nessie were really seeing a waterspout.

61 Dust devils are desert tornadoes. They shift tons of sand and cause terrible damage—they can strip the paintwork from a car in seconds!

▶ A whirling storm of sand in the desert.

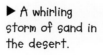

Pretty lights

62 **Rainbows are made up of seven colors.** They are caused by sunlight passing through falling raindrops. The water acts like a glass prism, splitting the light. White light is made up of seven colors—red, orange, yellow, green, blue, indigo, and violet—so these are the colors, from top to bottom, that make up the rainbow.

REMEMBER IT!

ROY G. BIV

Each letter of this name gives the first letter of each color of the rainbow—as it appears in the sky:

Red Orange Yellow
Green Blue
Indigo Violet

63 **Two rainbows can appear at once.** The top rainbow is a reflection of the bottom one, so its colors appear the opposite way round, with the violet band at the top and red at the bottom.

64 **Some rainbows appear at night.** They happen when falling raindrops split moonlight, rather than sunlight. This sort of rainbow is called a moonbow.

▲ Although a fogbow is colorless, its inner edge may appear slightly blue and its outer edge slightly red.

65 **It is not just angels that wear halos!** When you look at the Sun or Moon through a curtain of ice crystals, they seem to be surrounded by a glowing ring of light called a halo.

66 **Three suns can appear in our sky!** "Mock suns" are two bright spots that appear on either side of the Sun. They often happen at the same time as a halo, and have the same cause—light passing through ice crystals in the air.

▼ An aurora—the most dazzling natural light show on Earth!

▶ Mock suns are also known as parhelia or sundogs.

67 **Some rainbows are just white.** Fogbows happen when sunlight passes through a patch of fog. The water droplets in the fog are too small to work like prisms, so the arching bow is white or colorless.

▲ A halo looks like a circle of light surrounding the Sun or Moon.

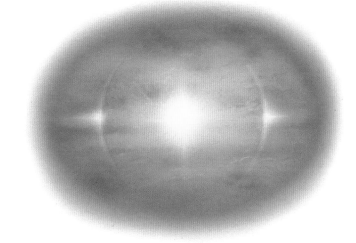

68 **Auroras are curtains of lights in the sky.** They happen in the far north or south of the world when particles from the Sun smash into molecules in the air—at speeds of 1,000mph (1,600km/h). The lights may be blue, red, or yellow.

Made for weather

69 **Camels can go for two weeks without a drink.** These animals are adapted to life in a hot, dry climate. They do not sweat until their body temperature hits 104°F (40°C), which helps them to save water. The humps on their backs are fat stores, which are used for energy when food and drink is scarce.

70 **Lizards lose salt through their noses.** Most animals get rid of excess salt in their urine, but lizards, such as iguanas and geckos, live in dry parts of the world. They need to lose as little water from their bodies as possible.

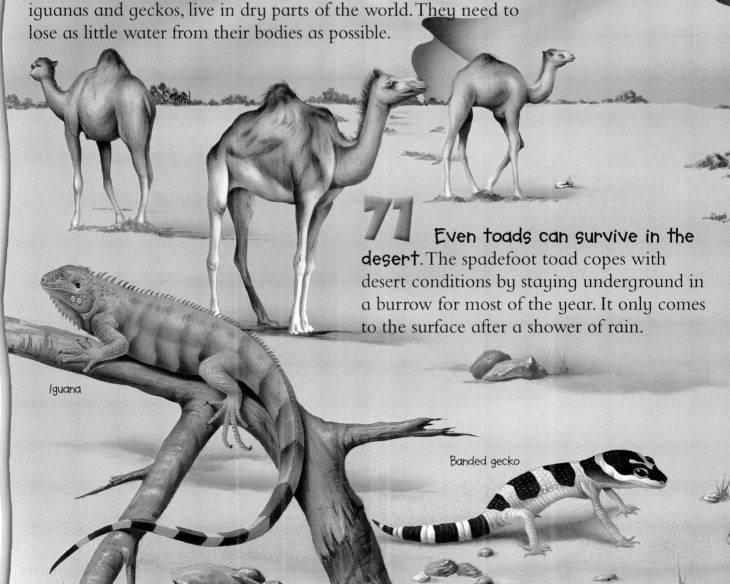

Camel

71 **Even toads can survive in the desert.** The spadefoot toad copes with desert conditions by staying underground in a burrow for most of the year. It only comes to the surface after a shower of rain.

Iguana

Banded gecko

▶ Beneath its gleaming—white fur, the polar bear's skin is black to absorb heat from the Sun.

QUIZ

Rearrange the letters to find the names of four plants that can cope with a very dry climate.
1. ROAGAUS SACCUT
2. OBABBA ETRE
3. YLPCIRK REAP
4. SCUYTPALUE

1. Saguaro cactus 2. Baobab tree 3. Prickly pear 4. Eucalyptus

◀ These animals have adapted to life in very dry climates. However, they live in different deserts around the world.

Spadefoot toad

72 **Polar bears have black skin.** These bears have all sorts of special ways to survive the polar climate. Plenty of body fat and thick fur keeps them snug and warm, while their black skin soaks up as much warmth from the Sun as possible.

73 **Acorn woodpeckers store nuts for winter.** Animals in temperate climates have to be prepared if they are to survive the cold winter months. Acorn woodpeckers turn tree trunks into larders. During the fall, when acorns are ripe, the birds collect as many as they can, storing them in holes that they bore into a tree.

▶ Storing acorns helps this woodpecker survive the cold winter months.

Weather myths

74 **People once thought the Sun was a god.** The sun god was often considered to be the most important god of all, because he brought light and warmth and ripened crops. The ancient Egyptians built pyramids that pointed up to their sun god, Re, while the Aztecs believed that their sun god, Huitzilpochtli, had even shown them where to build their capital city.

75 **The Vikings thought a god brought thunder.** Thor was the god of war and thunder, worshiped across what is now Scandinavia. The Vikings pictured Thor as a red-bearded giant. He carried a hammer that produced bolts of lightning. Our day, Thursday, is named in Thor's honor.

◀ In Scandinavian mythology, Thor was the god of thunder.

▲ The Egyptian sun god, Re, was often shown with the head of a falcon.

76 **Hurricanes are named after a god.** The Mayan people lived in Central America, the part of the world that is most affected by hurricanes. Their creator god was called Huracan.

77 Totem poles honored the Thunderbird. Certain tribes of Native Americans, built tall, painted totem poles, carved in the image of the Thunderbird. They wanted to keep the spirit happy, because they thought it brought rain to feed the plants.

▶ A Native American Indian totem pole depicting the spirit of the Thunderbird.

78 People once danced for rain. In hot places such as Africa, people developed dances to bring rain. These were performed by the village shaman (religious woman or man), using wooden instruments such as bullroarers. Sometimes water was sprinkled on the ground. Rain dances are still performed in some countries today.

◀ Shamans wore a special costume for their rain dance.

MAKE A BULLROARER

You will need:

wooden ruler   some string

Ask an adult to drill a hole in one end of the ruler. Thread through the string, and knot it, to stop it slipping through the hole. In an open space, whirl the instrument above your head to create a wind noise!

Rain or shine?

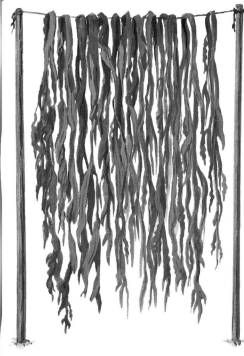

▲ Kelp picks up any moisture in the air, so it is a good way of telling how damp the atmosphere is.

79 **Seaweed can tell us if rain is on the way.** Long ago, people looked to nature for clues about the weather. One traditional way of forecasting was to hang up strands of seaweed. If the seaweed stayed slimy, the air was damp and rain was likely. If the seaweed shriveled up, the weather would be dry.

80 **"Red sky at night is the sailor's delight."** This is one of the most famous pieces of weather lore and means that a glorious sunset is followed by a fine morning. The saying is also known as "shepherd's delight." There is no evidence that the saying is true, though.

I DON'T BELIEVE IT!

People used to say that cows lay down when rain was coming—but there is no truth in it! They lie down whether rain is on the way or not!

81 **Groundhogs tell the weather when they wake.** Of course, they don't really, but in Pennsylvania, Groundhog Day is a huge celebration. On February 2, people gather to see the groundhog come out. If you see the creature's shadow, it means there are six more weeks of cold to come.

▼ A blood-red sunset is delightful to look at, but it can't help a sailor to predict the next day's weather.

▲ The Moon is clearly visible in a cloudless night sky. Its light casts a silvery glow over the Earth.

82 **"Clear moon, frost soon."** This old saying does have some truth in it. If there are few clouds in the sky, the view of the Moon will be clear—and there will also be no blanket of cloud to keep in the Earth's heat. That makes a frost more likely—during the colder months, at least.

83 **The earliest weather records are more than 3,000 years old.** They were found on a piece of tortoiseshell and had been written down by Chinese weather watchers. The inscriptions describe when it rained or snowed and how windy it was.

◀ Records of ancient weather were scratched on to this piece of shell.

Instruments and inventors

84 **The Tower of Winds was built 2,000 years ago.** It was an eight-sided building and is the first known weather station. It had a wind vane on the roof and a water clock inside.

85 **The first barometer was made by one of Galileo's students.** Barometers measure air pressure. The first person to describe air pressure—and to make an instrument for measuring it—was an Italian, Evangelista Torricelli. He had studied under the great scientist Galileo. Torricelli made his barometer in 1643.

▲ This is how the Tower of Winds looks today. It was built by Andronicus of Cyrrhus in Athens around 75BC. Its eight sides face the points of the compass: north, northeast, east, southeast, south, southwest, west, and northwest.

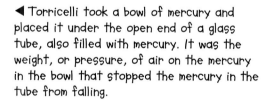

◄ Torricelli took a bowl of mercury and placed it under the open end of a glass tube, also filled with mercury. It was the weight, or pressure, of air on the mercury in the bowl that stopped the mercury in the tube from falling.

86 **Weather cocks have a special meaning.** They have four pointers that show the directions of north, south, east, and west. The cockerel at the top swivels so that its head always shows the direction of the wind.

▶ Weather cocks are often placed on top of church steeples.

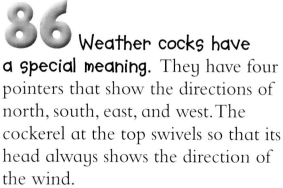

87

A weather house really can predict the weather. It is a type of hygrometer—an instrument that detects how much moisture is in the air. If there is lots, the rainy-day character comes out of the door!

▶ Weather houses have two figures. One comes out when the air is damp and the other when the air is dry.

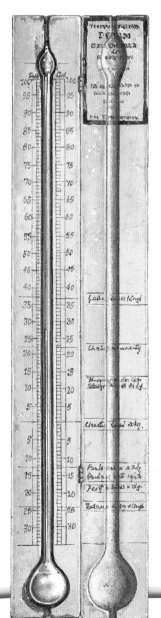

◀ This early thermometer shows both the Fahrenheit and the Celsius temperature scales.

88

Fahrenheit made the first thermometer in 1714. Thermometers are instruments that measure temperature. Gabriel Daniel Fahrenheit invented the thermometer using a blob of mercury sealed in an airtight tube. The Fahrenheit scale for measuring heat was named after him. The Centigrade scale was introduced in 1742 by the Swedish scientist Anders Celsius.

QUIZ

1. What is another name for the liquid metal, mercury?
2. What does an anemometer measure?
3. What does a wind vane measure?
4. On the Fahrenheit scale, at what temperature does water freeze?

1. Quicksilver 2. Wind speed 3. Wind direction 4. 32°F (0°C)

World of weather

89 **Working out what the weather will be like is called forecasting.** By looking at changes in the atmosphere, and comparing them to weather patterns of the past, forecasters can make an accurate guess at what the weather will be tomorrow, the next day, or even further ahead than that. But even forecasters get it wrong sometimes!

90 **The first national weather offices appeared in the 1800s.** This was when people realized that science could explain how weather worked—and save people from disasters. The first network of weather stations was set up in France, in 1855. This was after the scientist Le Verrier showed how a French warship, sunk in a storm, could have been saved. Le Verrier explained how the path of the storm could have been tracked, and the ship sailed to safety.

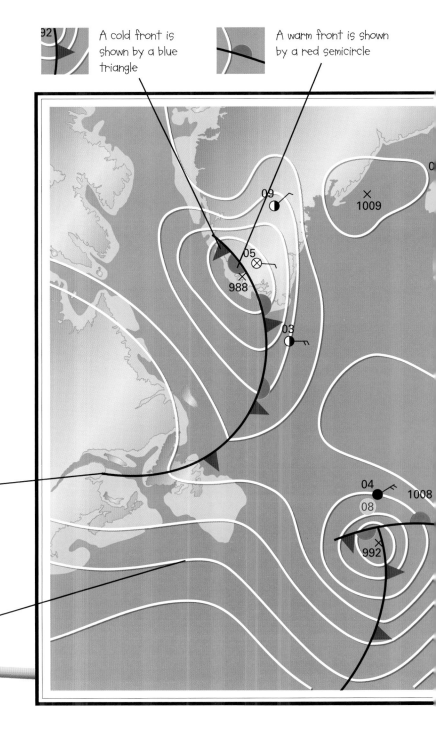

A cold front is shown by a blue triangle

A warm front is shown by a red semicircle

Look for the black lines with red semicircles and blue triangles—they represent an occluded front, where a cold front meets a warm front

These white lines are isobars—they connect places where air pressure is the same

WEATHER SYMBOLS

Learn how to represent the weather on your own synoptic charts. Here are some of the basic symbols to get you started. You may come across them in newspapers or while watching television. Can you guess what they mean?

91 Nations need to share weather data. By 1865, nearly 60 weather stations across Europe were swapping information. These early weather scientists, or meteorologists, realized that they needed to present their information using symbols that they could all understand. To this day, meteorologists plot their findings on maps called synoptic charts. They use lines called isobars to show which areas have the same air pressure. The Internet makes it easier for meteorologists to access information.

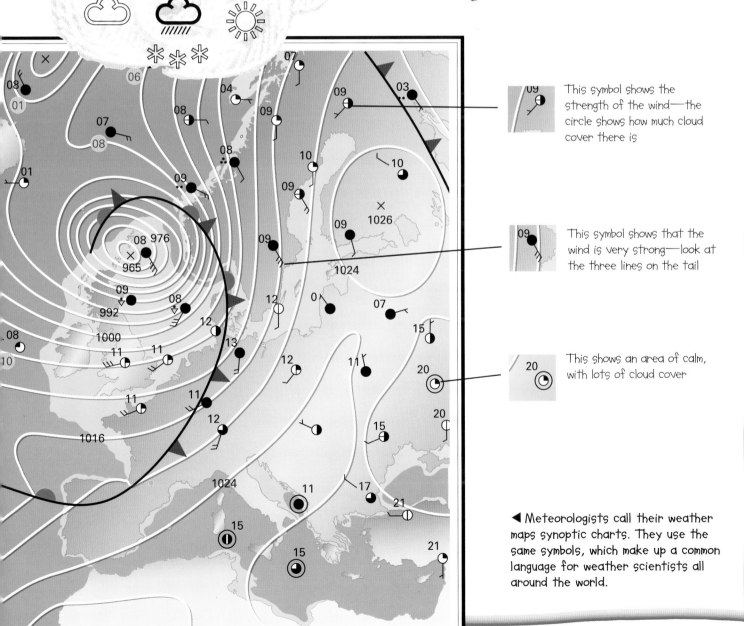

This symbol shows the strength of the wind—the circle shows how much cloud cover there is

This symbol shows that the wind is very strong—look at the three lines on the tail

This shows an area of calm, with lots of cloud cover

◄ Meteorologists call their weather maps synoptic charts. They use the same symbols, which make up a common language for weather scientists all around the world.

Weather watch

92 **Balloons can tell us about the weather.**
Weather balloons are hot-air balloons that are sent high into the atmosphere. As they rise, onboard equipment takes readings. These find out air pressure, and how moist, or humid, the air is, as well as how warm. The findings are radioed back to meteorologists on the ground, using a system called radiosonde. Hundreds of balloons are launched around the world every day.

▶ A weather balloon carries its scientific instruments high into the atmosphere.

93 **Some planes hound the weather.** Weather planes provide more atmospheric measurements than balloons can. *Snoopy* is the name of one of the British weather planes. The instruments are carried on its long, pointy nose, so they can test the air ahead of the plane.

▼ *Snoopy's* long nose carries all the equipment needed to monitor the weather.

94

Satellites help save lives. Their bird's-eye view of the Earth allows them to take amazing pictures of our weather systems. They can track hurricanes as they form over the oceans. Satellite-imaging has helped people to leave their homes and get out of a hurricane's path just in time.

I DON'T BELIEVE IT!

Some of the best weather photos have been taken by astronauts in space.

95

Some weather stations are all at sea. Weather buoys float on the surface of the oceans, measuring air pressure, temperature and wind direction. They are fitted with transmitters that beam information to satellites in space—which bounce the readings on to meteorologists. Tracking the buoys is just as important. They are carried along by ocean currents, which have a huge effect on our weather systems.

▲ A weather satellite takes photographs of Earth's weather systems from space.

► Currents carry the floating weather buoys around the oceans.

Changing climate

96 Climate change destroyed the dinosaurs —but no one can agree on what caused it. The best explanation is that a huge piece of space rock, called a meteorite, smashed into Earth. It threw up a giant cloud of dust that blocked out the Sun, plunging the world into cold and dark.

▼ Could a meteorite have crashed to Earth and changed the climate? A meteorite crater found in the Gulf of Mexico dates to 65 million years ago—exactly the time that the dinosaurs died out. Perhaps the impact changed the warm climate the dinosaurs were so used to.

▼ Vikings settled on Greenland's coastline. Inland areas were covered in ice.

97 Greenland used to be green! This island lies in the Arctic Ocean and is mostly covered by a huge ice sheet. Even in Viking times, Greenland was cold, but Viking settlers built at least two farming colonies there. These died out around the 1400s, after the climate cooled.

98 A volcano can change the climate!

Big volcanic explosions can create dust that blots out the Sun, just as a meteorite impact can. Dust from the 1815 eruption of a volcano called Tambora did this. This made many crops fail around the world and many people starved.

99 Tree felling is affecting our weather.

In areas of Southeast Asia and South America, rain forests are being cleared for farming. When the trees are burned, the fires release carbon dioxide—a greenhouse gas that helps to blanket the Earth and keep in the heat. Unfortunately, high levels of carbon dioxide raise the temperature too much.

◄ Like all plants, rain-forest trees take in carbon dioxide and give out oxygen. As rain forests are destroyed, the amount of carbon dioxide in the atmosphere increases.

100 Air temperatures are rising.

Scientists think the average world temperature may increase by around 2.7°F (1.5°C) this century. This may not sound like much, but the extra warmth means more storms, including hurricanes and tornadoes, and more droughts too.

QUIZ
1. What may have caused the death of the dinosaurs?
2. Which settlers once lived along the coast of Greenland?
3. Which gas do plants take in?

1. Meteorite impact 2. Vikings 3. Carbon dioxide

▶ Too much carbon dioxide in the atmosphere creates a 'greenhouse effect'. Just as glass traps heat, so does carbon dioxide. This means more storms and droughts.

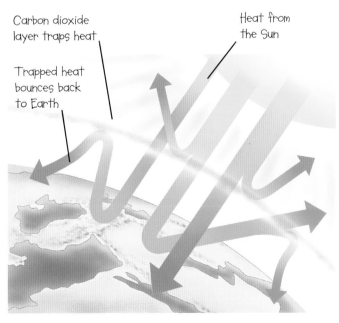

Carbon dioxide layer traps heat

Heat from the Sun

Trapped heat bounces back to Earth

Index

A B C
air **14**, **15**, 24
air pressure **15**, 24, 40
Antarctica 22, 23
atmosphere **14–15**
auroras **33**
avalanches **23**
barometer **40**
Beaufort Scale **25**
black ice **23**
bullroarers 37
camels, and the desert 34
carbon dioxide gas 47
Centigrade/Celsius scale 41
climate **6**, 46
clouds 14, **16–17**
　　types of **18–19**, 26
coldest place on Earth 22
contrails 19
currents, sea/ocean 13, 45
cyclones 28

D E F G
day 9
deserts 12, 20, 31
　　animals 34
　　peoples 12
droughts **13**
Dust Bowl 13
dust devils 31
Earth, orbit around Sun 8, 9
El Niño 13
electricity 24, 26
Fahrenheit scale 41
fogbows 32
floods 10, **20–21**
forecasting **38–39**, **42–43**
gods and goddesses 21, 36
Great Flood **21**
Greenland **46**
Groundhog Day 38

H I L M
hailstones 27
heat 12, 14
high pressure 15, 24
hottest place on Earth 12
Hurricane Hunters 28
hurricanes **28–29**
　　names 29, 36
hygrometer 41

ice crystals **22**
ice sheets 23, 46
lightning **26–27**
　　conductors 27
low pressure 15, 24
mackerel skies **19**
meteorologists 43, 44
Midsummer's Eve, Sweden 9
mirages **13**
monsoons **10**
Moon
　　and frost 39
　　halo **33**
moonbows 32
mountains 15, **16**, 21, 23
mudslides **21**

N O P R
Noah's ark 21
North Pole 6, 8, 9, 23
oxygen 15, 47
polar bear, black skin of 35
polar climate **6**
rain **16–17**
rain dances 37
rainbows **32–33**
rain forests 11, 47
rainy season 10, 11
radiosonde 44
red sky at night 39

S
Sahara, Africa 12
satellite-imaging 45
seasons **8–9**, **10–11**
seawater 16
seaweed, and forecasting 38
snow **22–23**
snowflakes **22**
snowslides 23
South Pole 6, 8, 23
stratosphere 14
summer 8, 9
Sun 8, 9, **12**, 13
　　halo **33**
sun gods 36
sunniest place on Earth 12
suns, mock (sundogs) **33**
synoptic charts 43

T
temperate climate **6**
temperature 16, 17
　　rising 47
temperature scales 41
thermometers **41**
Thunderbird 37
thunderclouds 30, 31
thunderstorms 20, **26–27**
　　calculating distance of 27
Tornado Alley, America 31
tornadoes **30–31**
totem poles 37
Tower of Winds 40
trade winds **24**, 25
tree felling 47
trees, change of leaf color 9
tropical climate **6**
tropical storms 20, 28
tropics **10**, **11**, 24
troposphere **14**, 15, 18
twisters 30
typhoons 28, 29

V W
virga **17**
volcanic explosions 47
water cycle **16**
water vapor 15, **16**, 17, 19
waterspouts **31**
waves, giant 29
weather **6–7**, 14
　　balloons **44**
　　buoys **45**
　　cocks 40
　　house 40
　　maps 43
　　planes 28, **44**
　　records, earliest (Chinese) 39
　　stations 40, **42**, 43
　　see also forecasting
wind turbines 24
winds **24–25**
　　measurement of 25
　　names 25
winter 8
woodpeckers, acorn 35

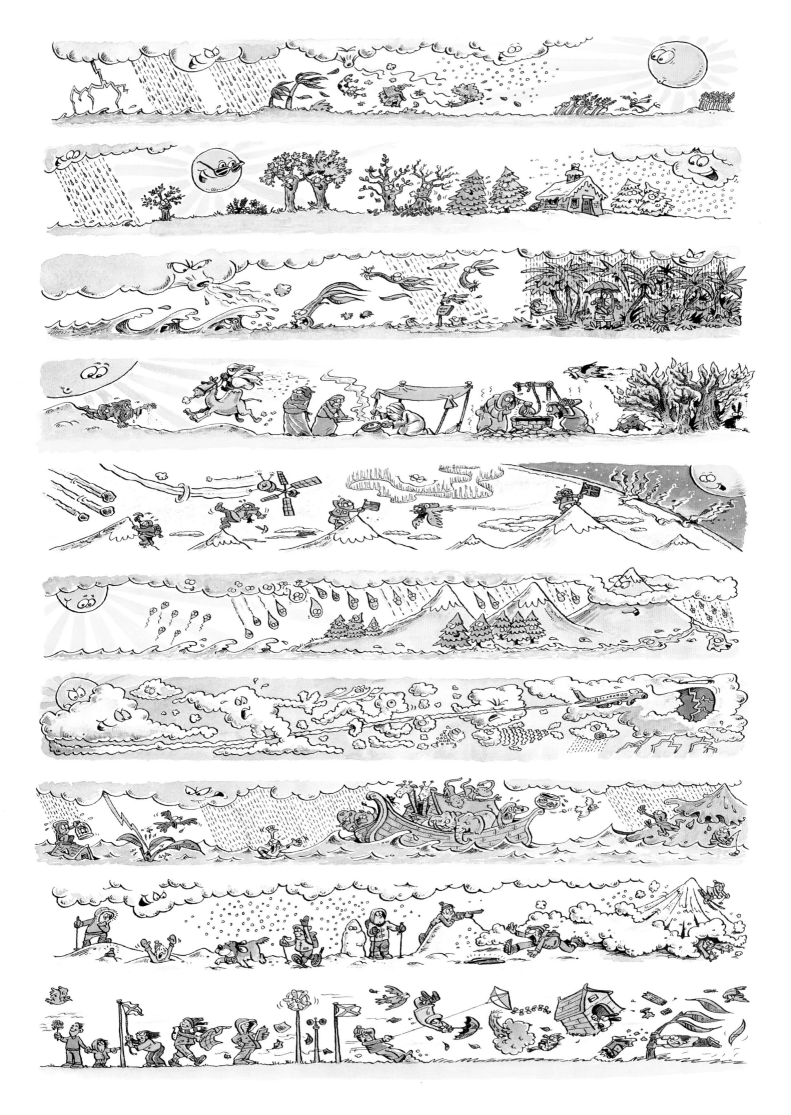